The Paleo Spiralizer Cookbook: Gluten-Free, Easy to Make, Irresistible Recipes That Will Help You Lose Weight & Look Great

Disclaimer and Terms of Use: Effort has been made to ensure that the information in this book is accurate and complete, however, the author and the publisher do not warrant the accuracy of the information, text and graphics contained within the book due to the rapidly changing nature of science, research, known and unknown facts and internet. The Author and the publisher do not hold any responsibility for errors, omissions or contrary interpretation of the subject matter herein. This book is presented solely for motivational and informational purposes only.

Table of Contents

Vegetable spiralizer recipes

Butternut squash noodles

Ingredients:
- 2 Butternut squash spiral cut, and soaked in water
- 1 package grape tomatoes
- 1 C carrots sliced
- 1 C green beans sliced
- ½ C mushrooms, diced
- ½ C red onion sliced
- ½ C red bell pepper chopped
- ½ C celery chopped
- 1 yellow squash, peeled and chopped

Curry:
- 1 C raw cashews
- 2 C coconut milk
- ¼ C coconut oil
- 1 inch ginger
- 2 tsp. curry
- Salt to taste
- Cayenne pepper to taste

Directions: You will use the spiralizer to make the noodles from the butternut squash. Soak in filtered water with salt while preparing vegetables.

In blender cup mix coconut curry ingredients until creamy. Drain noodles and more to pasta bowl. Top with vegetables and serve.

Dun dried Tomato Butternut squash

Ingredients:
- Butter nut squash pasta
- 4 medium organic fresh organic tomatoes
- ½ C sun dried tomatoes
- 2 fresh garlic cloves
- Lemon juice
- 1 tsp. dried herbs Provence
- ½ tsp sea salt
- ¼ tsp. pepper
- ½ C 100% pure avocado oil

Directions: Combine everything but the pasta in the food processor. Process for 30 seconds. Drizzle avocado oil over mix as its processing. This should take about 60 seconds in the processor total. Toss with butternut squash pasta.

Ingredients;
- 2 small zucchini, chopped (comes out to be two cups)
- ¼ tsp salt
- 1 T almond flour
- ½ tsp. coconut oil
- 1 T extra virgin olive oil
- 1 tsp. minced garlic
- 3 eggs scrambled

Directions: toss and salt the zucchini and let sit for about 20 minutes to drain. In medium to large skillet add almond flour, oil and little salt in skillet and sauté you want this a nice golden brown. This is your garnish for later. Put the pan back on the heat and add the noodles, sauté those for about 1-2 minutes. Next add lower the heat and add your eggs. Mix noodles and eggs, add garnish and serve.

Italian ball soup

Ingredients:

- 32 oz. beef broth
- 1 medium zucchini spiraled
- 2 sticks celery, chopped
- 1 Diced onion
- 1 medium tomato diced
- 1 carrot chopped
- 1 ½ tsp garlic salt
- 1 ½ ground beef uncooked
- ½ C parmesan cheese- shredded or grinded
- 4 tsp. minced garlic
- 1 egg
- 4 T fresh parsley
- 1 ½ tsp pepper
- 1 ½ tsp onion powder
- 1 tsp. Italian seasoning
- 1 tsp dried oregano

Directions: Heat broth, parmesan, garlic, egg salt, parsley, and other seasonings into your slow cook and set on low and cover. In bowl combine the meat and remaining ingredients and make small meatballs. Add to skillet and cook meatballs in the skillet. Add to slow cooker and cook for 6 hours.

Cucumber Spirals

Ingredients:
- 1-2 Cucumbers
- 1 radish

Directions: Run both through the spiralizer and toss with garnish and serve chilled

Red Salad

Ingredients:
- 4-6 beets
- Sunflower seeds
- 1-2 carrots

Directions: Run through the spiralizer and toss with the sunflower seeds already seeded) and serve chilled

Sweet potato salad

Ingredients:
- 1-2 sweet potatoes peeled
- Ginger dressing
- Crushed almonds

Directions: Run through the spiralizer and toss with the dressing and almonds. You can serve with slice tomatoes, or other vegetables.

Curly Fries

Ingredients:
- 3-4 potatoes
- Home seasoning
- Coconut oil

Directions: Spiral the potatoes into curly Q fries, and toss with house seasoning. Heat up oil in skillet and fry the potato curly Q fries, remove from grease and let cool.

Zucchini Wrap

Ingredients:
- Tortilla wraps
- 2 T hummus
- ¼ avocado sliced and spooned out
- Shredded carrots (about ½ C)
- ¼ C black beans
- 1 C zucchini pasta

Directions: start with the wrap start with spreading hummus in wrap, then avocado, carrots, beans, and noodles. Top with feta cheese and serve.

Cucumber Salad

Ingredients:
- 2 Cucumbers (blade B)
- ½ C diced red onions
- 1 C cherry tomatoes
- ½ T oregano
- 1 tsp garlic powder
- 1 T red wine vinegar
- 1 T olive oil
- 1/8 red pepper flakes
- 1/5 C baby spinach
- 1/3 C Kalamata olives
- ½ C chopped red bell pepper
- ¼ C crumbled feta
- ¼ C chickpeas

Directions: Add everything in a bowl and mix thoroughly to combine

Ingredients:
- 2 eggs
- ¼ C peanuts
- ½ T coconut oil
- 1 T minced garlic
- 1 minced shallot
- 1 T coconut flour
- 1 T chopped cilantro
- 2 zucchinis & blade C

Sauce:

- 2 T lime juice
- 1 T fish sauce
- ½ T soy sauce
- 1 T chili sauce
- 1 tsp honey

Directions: start with scrambling the eggs, and set to the side. Place all of the other ingredients into a bowl and start whisking together. Add the peanuts to the food processor and pulse or blend, nothing big should be left. Set everything aside, take a skillet over medium heat add oil and garlic and shallots, cook 1-2 minutes. Add sauce and whisk. Once thick add noodles and stir. Let simmer for about 2-3 minutes, add eggs and peanuts. Serve with lime.

Sausage and Asparagus

Ingredients:
- 2 T olive oil
- 2 lbs. sausage cooked and drained
- One sweet potato peeled and sliced blade C
- 1 garlic clove minced
- ¼ tsp red pepper flakes
- ½ C beef broth
- 2 T chopped parsley
- 6 Asparagus stalks

Directions: If you already have the sausage cooked, than set that aside and start cutting ends off the asparagus. You want to save both ends. Add everything to the sausage (which you had set aside hopefully) add broth and toss everything carefully, ass asparagus last. Noodles should be last, make sure soft and done, than serve.

Plantain rice and beans

Ingredients:
- 2 large plantains (blade C)
- 2 T olive oil
- 2 T minced garlic
- 3/4 C yellow onion
- ½ tsp adobo seasoning
- 1 tsp chili powder
- 1 Tsp cumin powder
- ½ C chicken broth
- 1 can whole tomatoes (peeled)
- 1 can black beans

Directions: Run plantains through spiralizer, and make rice than set aside. Place a skillet or sauce pan and start with your olive oil, add garlic and pepper flakes, cook for 30 seconds, and add onion. Add remaining spices, and beans.

Sweet potato rice

Ingredients:
- 1-2 large sweet potatoes, peeled and blade C
- 1 T oil
- ½ C diced onion
- ½ C beef broth
- 2 eggs beaten
- ½ C cooked peas
- 1 tsp soy sauce

Directions: Run potato thru processor. In skillet heat up the oil and add onion, let simmer on low for 2 minutes. Add salt and pepper to taste. Stirring add broth and stir. Let simmer. Add eggs and simmer. Add the potato rice and peas, fold them in.

Jicama Fried

Ingredients:
- 1 Jicama
- Olive oil
- 1 T onion powder
- 2 tsp cayenne powder
- 1 tsp chili powder

Directions: St your oven to 400 degrees, run jicama thru the spiralizer, and set string fries in container with a lid and add seasoning. Add lid and shake, getting all of the seasoning on the fries. Remove from container and add to baking sheet and bake for around 15 minutes or so.

Veggie Sandwich

Ingredients:
- 1 medium potato, Blade C
- ½ tsp garlic powder
- 1 ½ tsp olive oil
- 1 egg
- Onion ring slice
- 1 sliced tomato
- 1 piece kale
- ½ an avocado
- ¼ C crumbled feta cheese

Directions: In a large skillet, add your oil and sweet potato noodle, garlic, salt & pepper, cook for about 6 or 7 minutes, you want them to be a bright orange color. Add noodles in a bowl, crack raw egg over noodle. Coat the noodles, add ramekins, you want this to be about half way full, set in cool fridge for about 30 minutes, stir frequently make avocado cheese spread, and add to your noodles bowl with the avocado and set aside. Start layering as a sandwich.

Skinny ham and cheese sandwich

Ingredients:
- 1 sweet potato noodle
- 1 T olive oil
- Salt and pepper to taste
- 1 tsp garlic powder
- ½ C diced ham
- 1 egg
- ½ C shredded chees

Directions: Start with a skillet on medium heat, add potato noodles, and seasonings. Cook for about 8-10 minutes or until they are soft. Add the eggs, and cheese, and flip the pancake, add ham in the middle.

Apple salad

Ingredients:
- 1 C Kale
- ½ C apple slices
- 1.2 C zucchini slices
- 2 T raisins
- 2 T almonds

Vinaigrette:

- 1 T red wine vinegar
- 1 2 T olive oil
- 1 T sherry vinegar
- 1 T Dijon vinaigrette
- 2 T fresh lemon juice

Directions: Toss everything in slaw ingredients in a bowl and set aside. Add all vinaigrette in a bowl and whisk. Pour over slaw and store cold.

Carrot peanut sauce

Ingredients:
- ½ C minced garlic
- 1 T tamari
- ¼ tsp powdered ginger
- ½ tsp. rice vinegar
- ¼ C nut butters
- 1 T red pepper flakes
- ¼ C coconut milk
- 1 C snow peas
- 2 green onions

Directions: Add first 7 ingredients in a bowl and move to food processor. You want these all combined very well. Let the sauce sit while you make the noodles.

Spiral Baked Potato

Ingredients:
- 1-2 potatoes, Blade C
- Bacon bits
- Nonfat cheddar cheese
- Seasoning

Directions: Take shredded potato and shake with the seasoning, add melted cheddar cheese and top with bacon bits

Eggs Benedict

Ingredients:
- 1 large sweet potato blade C
- Olive oil spray
- ¼ tsp garlic powder
- 1 avocado cubed
- 3 large eggs
- 1 T chopped cilantro

Sauce:
- 2 egg yolks
- 1 T lemon juice
- ½ tsp sea salt
- 1 pepper and adobe sauce (Canned is fine)
- 3 T coconut oil

Directions: Start with setting your oven to 425 degrees, and place your noodles on the baking sheet and coat with spray. Season and top with avocado and roast for around 12 minutes. While that is baking add egg yolks, lemon juice peppers and salt, and blend. You want this to be thickened. Ake your eggs as preferred, and pour or place over baked sweet potato curls, and sauce.

Colored Apple treats

Ingredients:
- 1-2 green apples
- 2-3 red delicious apples
- Handful grapes

Directions: Using spiralizer curl the apples and toss in butter, bake at 250 for 7-10 minutes, these will be like an apple chip. Add grapes and you will have dried apples and raisins. Great after school snack.

Beef and Zucchini

Ingredients:
- 1 lbs. cooked, strained beef
- 1-2 Zucchini spirals (blade C)
- Nonfat or low sodium ragu

Directions: Start with the zucchini at the bottom, set aside. Mix ragu with cooked beef. Pour over zucchini. Serve, this should serve 2.

Sweet potato Kale salad

Ingredients:
- 1 Sweet potato pasta, Blade C

Dressing:

- ¼ C raw cashews
- 1 C raw spinach chopped
- ¼ C almond milk
- 1 T minced garlic
- ½ T lemon juice
- ½ tsp Dijon mustard

Directions: Make the dressing and set aside. Layer your salad with the spinach first, then toss with the dressing and top with sweet potato spirals

Bright Salad

Ingredients:
- 1-2Carrots Blade C
- 1-2 Cauliflowers Blade C
- Coconut curry
- Feta Cheese

Directions: Add everything together, top with feta cheese and serve

Made in the USA
Lexington, KY
26 February 2015